世界文化遗产

網師園

World Cultural Heritage

THE MASTER-OF-NETS GARDEN

古 吴 轩 出 版 社
GUWUXUAN PUBLISHING HOUSE

水情逸韵赞网师 （代序）

金学智

北宋著名山水画家郭熙，在《林泉高致》中曾这样抒写意愿："丘园养素，所常处也；泉石啸傲，所常乐也；渔樵隐逸，所常适也……尘嚣缰锁，此人情所常厌也！"他以整饬而又参差的文学语言，高度概括了世世代代文人画士的泉石膏肓、渔樵情结。南宋的史正志，也正是循着这一审美指向，在苏州建起了万卷堂，并名其圃曰"渔隐"。他侨寓丹阳，赋籍江都，却为何选址渔隐于苏，并自号"吴门老圃"？这，偶然之中有必然。

从中国隐逸文化史上看，苏州可说是一大渊薮。且不说孙武子曾以其慧眼睿智，择地隐居于吴，就从中古说起，汉有梁鸿，仰望东南，唱着《适吴诗》寻觅到苏州皋桥；晋有张翰，知幾地吟着《思吴江歌》归隐于鲈乡故园；唐有陆龟蒙，潜居甫里，号江湖散人，常泛舟遨游太湖，并自比于渔父……他们均堪称一代隐逸文化之代表。至北宋，更有开封籍的苏舜钦，来苏创构了名园沧浪亭，"置身沧浪上，日与沧浪亲"。因此，史正志的渔隐于苏，宋宗元在万卷堂故址进而建构网师园，网师园又一度名为"苏邻小筑"……都应看作是吴地隐逸文脉自南宋以来的必然延续，这是一种历史的积淀。

苏州，又是水文化之所钟。烟波万顷的太湖，吞吐着云岚变幻的七十二峰；河道纵横的古城，则是"绿浪东西南北水，红栏三百九十桥"。在这浩渺滉漾、流波潆洄的水域里，洪亮吉《网师园》咏道："太湖三万六千顷，我与此君同枕波。却羡水

西湾子里，输君先已挂渔蓑。"小诗既显现了吴地水文化的意蕴，又揭橥了网师隐于水的情旨，可谓探得骊珠。

网师园，是水文化和隐逸文化的交汇、集结之点。在网师园，水即是隐，隐即是水，水情逸韵，相与融和而为流动的画卷，而为展开的诗篇。

中部略呈方形、聚而不分的水池，是全园的主体、中心。它小中见大，芥纳须弥，表现出理水艺术的极致。环池景物不但小巧空灵，反衬出水面的"沧波渺然，一望无际"，而且无不聚焦着水之母题：月到风来亭，秀出于水；竹外一枝轩，直面于水；射鸭廊方亭，濒架于水；濯缨水阁，轻浮于水；起伏的游廊，傍卧于水；岸下的穴洞，虚受于水；参差的渔矶，浸贴于水……此外，池之周际，巽位有"涧深暗溜响"的源头以及水闸，乾位有"随波逝将去"的水尾，均拓展和活化着池水，还巧妙地创造出《园冶》"疏水若为无尽，断处通桥"的意境。源头的"槃涧"题刻，取典于《诗经·卫风·考槃》，寓有"退而穷处"、"隐于涧谷"之意，此为画龙点睛之笔；濯缨水阁，是又一点睛之笔，引出了《楚辞·渔父》中的《沧浪之歌》："沧浪之水清兮，可以濯吾缨……"一系列景构、意象足以说明：在风骚汇涵的网师园，水，乃是隐之体；隐，乃是水之魂。

西部的殿春簃庭院，似是旱园，其实不然。坤隅幽深的涵碧泉，是为活眼，它点醒了庭院荡漾的水意、纵横的逸趣；而冷泉亭则又为"涵碧"点题。至于满庭渔网纹的花街铺地，扇形图案中的莲花形象，更逗人萌生江湖之思。

东部宅第建筑和全园其他建筑附属的工艺、装饰，又从另一侧面沾溉于"水"之精神。像昆曲"腔用水磨"一样，网师园"藻耀高翔"门楼的繁富，"竹松承茂"门楼的简洁，万卷堂陈设的高雅，小姐楼家具的精致，殿春簃花窗的巧丽，梯云室落地罩的细腻……乃至网师园整体地作为一个精品园，也都离不开精推细敲、精雕细琢的水磨工夫。这和渔樵情结、隐逸趣尚似是对立的，但又是统一的，二者统一于水之精神，统一于"诗意地栖迟"，统一于"城市山林"互生互补的情韵之美。

网师园的题额，还有"网师小筑"、"潭西渔隐"、"樵风径"、"可以栖迟"、"岩腹涧唇"、"琴室"、"真意"等。它引领人们进入神思的空间、诗乐的天地，从而似已置身于山道樵径，徜徉于湖滨泽畔，踽踽焉，洋洋焉，耳际如闻古琴名曲《渔樵问答》，悠扬的琴音，如应如和，轻韵缓度；又似断续响起彭启丰的《网师小筑吟》："物谐厥性，人乐其天。临流结网，得鱼忘筌……踔尔幽赏，烟波浩然。江湖余乐，同泛吴船。"这已臻于物我两忘、天人合一的境界。

在网师园，悠悠水情，恬恬逸韵——人的志趣，在这里得以脱俗，得以涤尘；人的性灵，在这里受到洗礼，受到提升！

2002 年 12 月

THE GARDEN WITH GRACE OF WATERS

By Jin Xuezhi

Guo Xi, a well-known landscape painter of the Northern Song Dynasty, so describes his sentiment in *The Realm of Forests and Springs*: "Always prefer a garden to cultivate the mind and to live in, lofty mountains and waters to inspire the heart, seek the pleasure and comforts of the fisherman and woodcutter, and stay away from the moil of hectic city life that imprison the mind!" The explicit and paradoxical literary language summarizes the innate craving of the literary elite in ancient times for the beauty of nature and their aloofness of recluse symbolized by the fisherman and woodcutter. It is motivated by this aesthetic judgment that Shi Zhengzhi of the Southern Song Dynasty, born in Yangzhou and posted in Jiangdu for official duties, chose to retire and build his "Hall of Ten Thousand Volumes" in Suzhou and named it "Fisherman's Retreat". Traditionally, Suzhou has been a fond destination in the phenomenon of Chinese literati-recluses. The earliest instance is Sun Wu of the Spring and Autumn Period, who wrote his world-famous *Art of War* in his hermitage in Suzhou. In later times, there were Liang Hong of the Han dynasty, Zhang Han of the Jin dynasty who resigned from official post to retire to his birthplace Wujang, Lu Guimeng, the poet of the Tang, and poet Su Shunqing of the Northern Song dynasty, who came to Suzhou to create his Surging Waves Pavilion, etc. The former site of the Fisherman's Retreat was renovated by Song Zongyuan of the Qing period and renamed the Master-of-nets Garden, also known as Neighboring Garden of the Su's on account of its closeness to the Surging Waves Pavilion. There is a consistent historical trend for the scholar-gentry to make Suzhou their ultimate choice in search of retreat.

Water is the essence of the culture in Suzhou: the expansive Lake Tai with 72 islands and cloud-wrapped hills, the intricate web of waterways and canals inside the ancient city described in poetry as "green ripples spread in all directions linking three hundred and ninety bridges of red-painted railings." The poet Hong Liangji, in his *Master-of-nets Garden,* thus addresses the owner of the garden in envious tones: "On the mighty Lake Taihu, you and I shared the pleasure of rowing on the waves, yet now you beat me with your delicate cove of waters, in which to enjoy the ease of the fisherman."The poem artfully reveals that water is not only the cultural background of the region, but also the underlying theme of the garden.

The Master-of-nets Garden is the embodiment of water-associated culture and reclusive culture. Each is found in the other as if in an unfolded picture, or a poem being recited.

The rectangle central part of the garden is focused on a pool of water serving as the main element of the overall layout. A masterly stroke in water crafting, the pond gives the illusion of expanses of flowing streams, a reflection of a much bigger world in a nutshell. The buildings around the pond, small in scale and open to deeper vistas beyond them, are so conceived as to heighten the predominant theme of water: the Pavilion of Breeze in Moon-lit Night towers over the water; the Bamboo-flanked Pavilion faces the water; the square pavilion of the Duck-hunting Veranda extends across the water; the Water-side Pavilion of Washing Hat Tassel is floating over the water; and the undulating corridor nestles along the water; the caves along the shoreline give way to streams; and the overhanging rocky edges almost touch the water... Besides, on the southeast, there was a sluice gate to suggest the source of the stream, while in the northwest a downstream indicates the direction of a river course. All this is a vivid exemplification of the principle, "bridges are designed at the edge of water to suggest endless flow," in Ji Cheng's classic work *On Garden Creation*. The inscription "Panjian" at the supposed fountainhead was taken from ancient poetry to suggest that the stream was hidden in a mountain ravine. The name of Water-side Pavilion of Washing Hat Tassel brings to mind the famous lines in *Song of Surging Waves*: "When the water of the surging waves runs clear, I wash my hat tassel in it." The scenes and implications in the garden all point to the quintessence of the garden motif: water and retirement.

In the west lies the courtyard of Peony Cottage, which, in seeming scarcity of water, is focused on the water theme. Green

bridges ✓   wood carving ✓
winding corridors   Terraces ✓
moon-shaped door-frames   mirrored ✓
scrolls, art, vases   Rockery ✓
antique ceramics
Brick-carved doorways   pavings ✓
                          grounds

Spring is a small pool of gushing spring with rocky edges and the nearby Pavilion of Cold Spring is named after it. The mosaic paving in the court bear the pattern of fishing nets, and the lotus flower pattern in the fan-shaped cobble paving also calls to mind rivers and lakes.

The residential quarters in the eastern section, including the artwork and decorations, also touch upon the theme of water. The ornate brick-carved doorway with the inscription "Soaring Literary Accomplishment", another brick-carved gateway with the inscription "Thriving Bamboo and Pines" in a style of simplicity, the elaborate furnishings inside the boudoir upstairs, the delicate flower windows inside the Peony Cottage, the fine woodwork on the circular floor screen in the Hall of Cloud Stairway, etc., have been the result of the most meticulous and well-polished handwork. Seemingly contradictory to the notion of the retired fisherman, these adornments serve to complement the poetic ease and leisure in appreciation of the "mountains and forests" and idealized nature in the urban surroundings.

Inscriptions in the garden cast evocative light to the prospects: Small Cottage of the Fishing Master, the Fisherman's Retreat west of the Pond, Mountain Path of the Woodcutter, Cliff Edge and Mouth of Stream, the Lute Chamber, and True Sense, etc. They incite the visitor's imagination and deepen his contemplation and appreciation of the world of music and poetry. One seems to find himself on the mountain path, or by the splashing waters of a lake as a solitary stroller, or boating in the great lakes of the Wu Region. Here, man and nature are blended into one harmony.

The tranquility and ease of mind found in the Master-of-nets Garden, coupled by the scenes of waters, purifies the mind and elevates it to a level of sublimity, and from here, man will derive boundless pleasure.

小园极则

潘益新

网师园位于苏州古城东南阔家头巷，全园面积不足九亩，是一座典型的宅第园林。园内建筑秀雅，装饰精美，花木多姿，山水入画，奥旷兼得，曲折幽深，尤宜于静观，被誉为苏州园林之"小园极则"、以少胜多的典范。1982年被国务院列为全国重点文物保护单位。1997年被联合国教科文组织列入《世界文化遗产名录》。

网师即渔翁，网师园意谓"渔夫钓叟之园"。据清钱大昕《网师园记》，园为南宋淳熙间侍郎史正志万卷堂故址，有花圃，名"渔隐"。清乾隆中叶，光禄寺少卿宋宗元养母归隐时重建，借"渔隐"原意自比渔翁，始称网师园。乾隆末年归瞿远村，俗称"瞿园"。由于瞿氏巧为运思，使网师园"地只数亩，而有纡回不尽之致；居虽近廛，而有云水相忘之乐"。清同治中归李鸿裔。因与宋代苏舜钦名园沧浪亭相近，更园名为"苏邻小筑"。李工诗文书法，精于鉴赏，今园中尚存其手书诗文刻石十二方。清光绪末，归达桂，经修葺后复名"网师园"。入民国，张作霖购得此园，易名"逸园"，于1917年赠其师张锡銮。抗日战争前，金石书画家叶恭绰和国画大师张大千、张善子昆仲借寓园中。其时名流荟萃，诗画雅集，觞咏留题，极一时之盛。1940年，园归文物鉴藏家何亚农，整修后复"网师"旧名。1950年，其后人将园献给国家。1958年10月，经整修后对游人开放。

网师园大体可分三个部分。东部为宅第。有前后三进，严整规范，呈中轴对称格局。正门南有照壁，东、西两侧有辕门。进门为门厅。再进为主厅万卷堂，是举行隆重礼仪活动的场所，屋宇高敞，庄严肃穆。堂前的砖细门楼雕镂精致，镌有"文王访贤"、"郭子仪上寿"戏文故事，使小院洋溢着福、禄、寿、德的祥和气氛。堂后内厅撷秀楼为女眷燕集、起居之所。厅后小门可通梯云室，西侧可达园池。宅第东侧有一狭窄长弄，从门厅直达内厅，乃为女眷和仆役行走而设，故称避弄。门厅西侧有小门，额曰"网师小筑"，由此可直接入园。

中部为园池。以水池为中心，分环池和南、北三个景区。池南为昔日园主燕居雅聚之所，小山丛桂轩、蹈和馆、琴室形成一组幽深曲折、委宛有致的小院落。小山丛桂轩为四面厅结构，玲珑空透，环以檐廊，为一主要建筑。轩南有湖石花台，上植丛桂，寓招隐之意。轩北有黄石假山遮挡，与中部水池相隔。出小院循廊北进，豁然开朗，为全园重点景区。该区以池水为中心，环以轩廊亭阁、山石花木。池仅半亩许，略呈方形，聚而不分，以显其宽。四周建筑低临水面，黄石池岸凹凸曲折，池东南和西北隅各有溪涧、水湾，藏源隐尾，给人以水广波延、源远流长之感。池南濯缨水阁面水傍崖，最宜盛夏纳凉观鱼，与其东古朴质厚的"云岗"假山组成池南景观。池西有月到风来亭，踞于水涯高处，为园内主景，最宜赏月。池东北有方亭、射鸭廊、竹外一枝轩，连成高低错落的建筑群，与月到风来亭互为对景。竹外一枝轩院内修竹摇绿，轩前松梅相依。于此凭栏南望，石矶贴水，拱桥微露，池内天光山色、廊阁花树，倒影如画。

池北有五峰书屋、集虚斋、看松读画轩，构成以读书、颐养为主要功能的庭院一区。这些高大建筑均退隐于后，与水池间或亘以假山花台，或隔以小院矮轩，若隐若现，既有效地扩大了池面，又增加了园景的层次与深度。看松读画轩清雅素朴，建筑精绝，前后及左侧均为天井小院，栽花木、垒石峰构成窗景。轩前古柏树龄已逾八百年，老而弥坚，苍然耸翠，相传为南宋史正志手植。轩东有集虚斋，楼上檐廊朱栏，可凭可依，一园美景尽收眼底。中、新合作苏州工业园区建设谈判，曾多次在此举行。

西部为内园，即殿春簃庭院。此地原为芍药圃，一春花事，以芍药殿后，故名。"簃"为昔日园主内书房，环境清幽，最宜读书。院内峰石嶙峋，铺地整洁，花容绰约。西南冷泉亭依墙而筑，旁有涵碧泉。屋后窗景，别致幽雅。殿春簃庭院颇具明代园林疏旷柔和、雅淡明快、工整而简洁的特色。在美国纽约大都会艺术博物馆建造的中国式庭院"明轩"，即以殿春簃为范本，开创了苏州园林艺术分翠海外之先河。

综观园内建筑，以秀丽、精致、小巧见长，池周轩廊亭阁，更有小、低、透的特点。室内家具陈设也精美多致，古雅可爱，并不乏明清红木珍品。几案摆件，则尤以所藏古瓷为佳，其工艺精湛、造型优美、色泽莹润，亦为苏州园林所仅见。每当夜幕低垂，华灯初上，网师园内轻歌曼舞，弦管悠扬，典雅的昆曲、评弹，令无数中外来宾倾倒。连续举办十余年的古典夜园游活动，已成为苏州的特色旅游项目。

清人张问陶《游网师园》云："何止画图开绣轴，真从城市见桃源。"历经几代人的精心养护，网师园如绣轴，似桃源，成为小巧精致雅丽的历史名园。今天，大步走向世界的网师园，热忱欢迎来自海内外的朋友，欢迎来此人间仙境，走进这锦绣画卷深处。

THE CLASSIC MODEL OF DELICATE GARDENS

By Pan Yixin

The Master-of-nets Garden, located in Kuojiatou Lane in the southeast of the ancient city of Suzhou, is a typical residential garden with a meager area of one and half acres. The elegant and delicate buildings, exquisite decorations, diverse vibrant vegetation, picturesque and intricate scenes through ever-changing perspectives, are worth savoring in a tranquil atmosphere. Acknowledged to be the classic model of delicate classical gardens of Suzhou, the garden exemplifies the concept of "the few outshines the many" in landscape gardening. It was listed by the State Council in 1982 as a cultural relic at national level, and in 1997, UNESCO put the garden in the registrar of World Cultural Heritage.

The name of the garden denotes "the garden of the fisherman". According to *Record on Master-of-nets Garden* by Qian Daxin of the Qing dynasty, Shi Zhengzhi, Vice-minister of finance during the Chunxi Reign of the Southern Song dynasty, first built his Hall of Ten Thousand Volumes here, with an attached pleasure garden named "Fisherman's Retreat". In the mid-Qing period, Song Zongyuan, a protocol official, rebuilt the garden for his mother in recuperation, and to echo the implication of the fisherman, he named it the Master-of-nets Garden. In the late Qianlong Reign, the garden belonged to Qu Yuancun, and was called Qu's Garden. Under his creative renovation, the garden "offers intricate scenic prospects and, though in an urban setting, affords the pleasure in a natural lake." During the Tongzhi Reign, Li Hongyi acquired the garden and changed its name into "Neighboring Cottage to Su's" on account of its location in the vicinity of the famous Surging Waves Pavilion created by Su Shunqing of the Song period. Li, a literary celebrity well versed in poetry and calligraphy, has left twelve engraved stone tablets of poems in the garden to this day. In the late Guangxu Reign, the garden went into the hands of Da Gui, who again renovated the garden and restored its name, the Master-of-nets Garden. In the period of the Republic, Zhang Zuolin bought the garden and renamed it the Garden of Ease, and gave it to his teacher Zhang Xiluan in 1917 as a gift. Before the World War II, the garden was lent to Ye Gongzhuo, an artist of seal engraving, calligraphy, and painting, and the master artist Zhang Daqian and his brother Zhang Shanzi for residence. During these years, the garden became a glamorous gathering place for celebrated scholars and artists of the time, and many valuable works were left from that period. In 1940, the garden came to the possession of He Yanong, a curio connoisseur, who restored both the garden and its original name. His descendents donated the garden to the Government after Liberation, and it was opened to the public after repair in October 1958.

The garden consists chiefly of three parts. The eastern section is the residential quarters in symmetrical progression of three courts along a central axis. The main entrance faces a screen wall flanked with east and west gateways. The entrance hall is followed by a spacious and stately hall, the Hall of Ten Thousand Volumes, where important ceremonies used to be held. In the forecourt of the hall is an ornate brick-carved doorway, on which theatrical figures recount the stories of "King Wen Visits the Sage", and "General Guo Ziyi's Birthday", etc., adding an auspicious atmosphere of "happiness, fortune, and longevity" to the enclosure. The Hall of Capturing Grace behind the main hall, the reception hall for ladies, leads to the Hall of Cloud Stairway, and a small door on one side allows for a garden backdrop. Along the left side of the living quarters, a long narrow alleyway runs from the entrance hall to the interior, as a walkway for servants. A side door marked with the name of the garden on the west of the entrance hall also gives direct access to the garden.

The focal point of the garden is a central pond with surrounding scenes. To the south is a small quiet court enclosed by the Hall of Osmanthus Hill, Taohe Hall, and Lute Chamber. The rectangular Hall of Osmanthus Hill, with windows on four sides, is the major building in this compound affording views from all directions, and is approached by a covered walk. Opposite to the hall is a rock-rimmed flowerbed grown with osmanthus trees, symbolizing "beckoning to the retired" according to a literary allegory. The northern side of the hall is screened off by a granite hillock from the central pond.

The corridor leads northward from the small court to the major landscape of the garden dominated by a square central pond roughly edged with rocks. Instead of being straddled with buildings, the water is a converging body from all directions, whereas brooklets and coves at the southeast and northeast edges heighten the illusion of a natural flow with an outside source. With rocky edges and concaves, the pond is made to seem larger because its irregular shape cannot be seen all at once. The buildings around the pond are all laid out close to the water. The Water-side Pavilion of Washing Hat Tassel to the south, an ideal spot for watching fishes and enjoying cool breeze in summer, along with the sturdy rocky hill "Cloud Ridge" on the east, forms the landscape on the southern shore. The Hall of Breeze in Moon-lit Night on the west of the pond, erected gracefully over the water, is a delightful resting place for appreciating the moon. On the northeast are the Square Pavilion, the Duck-hunting Veranda, and the Bamboo-flanked Pavilion, forming an architectural group in varying heights juxtaposed with the Hall of Breeze in Moon-lit Night across the pond. Looking southward from the Bamboo-flanked Pavilion, with pines and plum trees in front and bamboos in the adjacent court behind, the visitor will be enthralled by a serene picture of hills, buildings, delicate arch bridges, and flowering shrubs mirrored in the rock-edged pool.

To the north of the pond, a group of large-sized functional buildings (the Five Peaks Library, the Study Room of Accumulated Void, and the Hall of Viewing Pines and Contemplating Paintings) is set back from the pond behind flowerbeds, rocks, and tiny courts, half-concealed but adding depth to the garden prospects. The Hall of Viewing Pines and Contemplating Paintings, a quaint and elegant work of architecture, adjoins small courts on four sides in which flowers and rocks are framed through the fretwork windows. The ages-old verdurous cypress trees in front were planted by Shi Zhengzhi, the founder of the garden some eight hundred years ago. The Study Room of Accumulated Void is on the east of the hall, and the chamber and balustrade on the upper floor command a panoramic glimpse of the garden. It is in this very chamber that talks on the development of Sino-Singapore Suzhou Industrial Park was held on many occasions.

On the westernmost side is the inner garden named Peony Court, where peony flowers once dominated the scene. The quiet hall used to be the study room of the owner. The courtyard is adorned with rocks and elaborate mosaic paving. On the southwest is the Pavilion of Cold Spring and next to it is the Green Spring. Windows facing the backcourt are typical picture frames. The whole compound, typical of the style of extreme simplicity in the Ming dynasty, is the prototype by which the Ming Hall was built in the Metropolitan Museum of Art in New York City, the first instance of export of Suzhou classical gardens.

The buildings in the garden are delicate, elegant, and small in scale, especially the pavilions and corridors around the pond, which are moderately low in small proportions, and open to different perspectives. The interior furnishings are quaint and elaborate, some being valuable mahogany furniture of the Qing period. The table ornaments feature antiquated ceramics of excellent workmanship.

For over a dozen years, the classical night garden tour has been staged in this enchanting environment as a special tourist item. Classical music, Kunqu Opera, and the local ballad singing, folk dances have fascinated many guests from China and overseas.

In the prose *Touring the Master-of-nets Garden*, the author Zhang Wentao of the Qing dynasty remarks: "Like a scroll of painting and embroidery, a Shangri-la of dream is finally found in an urban setting." Perfected with the efforts of generations, the garden is winning an increased repute worldwide. Friends from all over the world are welcome to experience the thrill of this living landscape scroll.

大门前侧景观

The flank of the main entrance.

东、西各有外门，正南设有照壁，蟠槐垂舒浓荫，
显耀门庭华盖碧。

大门正面景观

The front of the main entrance.

红灯笼，高门槛。阀阅焜
耀，厅堂焕赫，宅第显贵门庭
深。

门厅及全景图

The entrance hall and picture of overall garden layout.

　　厅内《网师逸韵》图上，祥云缭绕，山水清朗，花木锦绣，楼阁轩昂，给人以身临仙境的第一印象。

厅前天井砖额
Inscriptions on brick portal in front of the Hall.

"锁云"，清王文治（1730—1802，梦楼）书
"锄月"，清冯桂芬（1809—1874）书

轿厅(门厅)内红木"竹舆轿"
The mahogany sedan chair in the entrance hall.

　盝顶红木仿竹节官轿，造型典重，雕镂细
密，乃显现姑苏工艺审美风格之杰构。

"藻耀高翔" 门楼
Brick-carved doorway inscribed
with "Soaring Literary
Accomplishment".

　屋顶，以翼角高翔为美；檐
下，以砖细藻饰为美——精雕细
琢，绝技无双，不愧"江南第一门
楼"！

门楼砖雕细部
The carved doorway and details in the
eastern section.

门楼融浮雕、圆雕、微雕、透雕、多层雕等于一体；方寸内刻
"郭子仪上寿"戏文，戏台空间进深有七八层之多！

椅旎网际园裹游侣如云

主厅万卷堂内景
The interior of the main hall, the Hall of Ten Thousand Volumes.

　　黑与白为主色调，明式家具，简洁大方，显现出朴素恬淡的渔隐意念，呈示出虚疏散朗的明代风格。

万卷堂次间长窗光影
Sunlight through the windows at the back of the Hall of Ten Thousand Volumes.

系列窗棂，以海棠变奏为巧，以连续齐一为美。日光穿窗入室，在地上织出空间的韵律。

堂上诸葛铜鼓
Bronze Zhuge Drum inside the hall.

堂内供石
Ornamental rock inside the hall.

如吉祥云之隆起而中空，如璎珞石之饱绽而奔涌；淙淙泻月，琅琅散珠。蟠蟠瑞霞，叠叠奇峰，为不可多得之"石清供"。

堂内大理石系列挂屏
Interior ornament of marble wall hangings.

寒泉锄月(冬)
Cold spring water under the moon
(winter).

白露横江(秋)
Mist over the river
(autumn).

华岳云深(夏)
Holy mountains clad in clouds
(summer).

春山晴翠(春)
Mountains in spring sunshine
(spring).

"竹松承茂"门楼
A doorway with the inscription,
"Thriving Pines and Bamboo".

如竹之茂，如松之盛，又有化繁为简之妙。砖雕寥寥，与"藻耀高翔"门楼形成简与繁、朴与丽、直与曲的审美对照。

撷秀楼内景
The interior of the Hall of Capturing Grace.

陈设典雅，装修精丽。在暖色氛围反衬中，
绿色的"撷秀"匾额耐人寻味。

"云窟"西院红枫

The red maple in the western court of
the compound Cloud Cave.

叶绚寒秋，如烧非因火；锦耀朱殷，似花不待春。缘何色酡心醉？
只因热恋园林美。

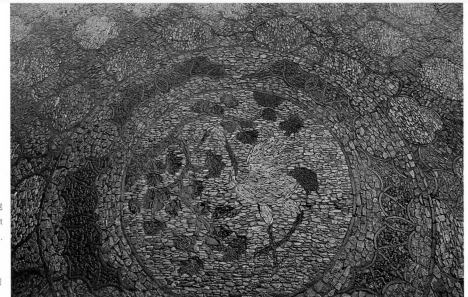

五峰书屋东院铺地
The mosaic paving in the eastern court
of the Five Peaks Library.

群蝠环拱，古松倒垂，起鹤舞而翩
跹，俨然一帧工笔翎毛画，妙不可言。

殿春簃庭院铺地
The mosaic paving in the Peony Court.

莲叶油油绿、荷花淡淡红。四周
毫无尘土气，只缘身在水云乡中。

梯云室落地罩
The floor frame inside the Hall of Cloud Stairway.

双钱、"百吉"、"卐"字，缠以藤茎，饰以梅雀，细、匀、密、齐、光、薄、曲、秀、和、精……众美皆备。

五峰书屋东侧楼山
The rockery on the east of the
Five Peaks Library.

湖石叠摞楼山高，岩穴中空，梯云
有磴道。画楼东侧门半掩，斯人未起，
枕上卧听松涛。

梯云室门框对景
Viewed through the doorframe of the Hall Cloud Stairway.

峰石花树、玲珑葱蒨烂熳，透过落地罩和门框外望，犹如雕饰华美的系列画屏。

室内"东坡题跋"木刻挂屏

The wooden wall hanging inscribed with "Dongpo's Postscript" inside the room.

清刘墉(1719—1804)书。宋代文豪巨儒,清代"浓墨宰相",诗、书艺术结良缘,雅韵逸趣深长。

梯云室长窗及裙板雕刻

The window panels and woodwork of the Hall
of Cloud Stairway.

"门扇岂异寻常，窗棂遵时各式。"落地长窗，对称而整齐；
裙板木雕，典雅而精丽。

繁盛的枸骨
The luxuriant evergreen holly.

树干硕壮,树冠繁敷;朱
实离离，绿叶簇簇——欣欣
分向荣，四季长青鸟不宿。

楼山东侧庭院
The courtyard on the east
side of the rockery.

古松疏疏绿，腊梅
澄澄黄，掩映着朱户绮
窗，隐隐沁出春光。

正屋东侧"避弄"

The side alleyway on the east of the
living quarters.

作为宅第园林之典范，网师园此
狭弄连贯三进，直通后花园，供女眷、
仆婢行走，以避男宾与主人。

中部水池景观
The scene around the central pond.

水池周边建筑, 小巧轻盈、低亚空灵, 反衬出"沧波渺然, 一望无际"的意境。

雪中亭
The pavilion after snowfall.

小桥横针，秀亭翼然飞举……白雪无不随
物而赋形，堆塑出粉装玉琢的世界。

镜中景
A mirrored scene.

　亭中镜映出池东景观，拓展并深化着
园林空间，令人感到似熟还生、似真实幻、
如同发光的水晶天地、琉璃画面。

雾中影

A scene in mist.

　　晨雾溟濛——风亭轻
锁，水阁淡笼；近桥沾湿，
远树消融；墨韵图淋漓渗
化，蒸腾为不可名状的梦。

池南二乔玉兰
Magnolias to the south of the pond.

玉树临风。枝头疏疏密密花，质如美玉琢就，色似水彩晕染；
其枝走笔如画，相交"女"字，密处留眼。

竹外一枝轩
The Bamboo-flanked Pavilion.

以苏轼"竹外一枝斜更好"诗意命名。雅致的斜轩中，廊庑曲折、朱栏透漏，门窗空灵，处处有可赏的美景。

竹外一枝轩窗景

The picture window in the Bamboo-flanked Pavilion.

"尺幅窗，无心画。"轩廊各式空窗，其对景无不是优美的画面：
或花树扶疏，小桥曲折；或华阁浮水，清流见底……

集虚斋前庭月洞门南望
Through the moon gate of the
forecourt of the Hall of
Accumulated Void.

团栾的月洞门，中含画
栏、云岗、花树、华轩……宛
同仙境广寒宫，可谓"超以象
外，得其环中"。

竹外一枝轩后庭
The backcourt of the Bamboo-flanked Pavilion.

月洞门中，长窗、铺地均作冰裂纹，其间竹影婆娑，摇曳出"岁寒长青"的主题。

集虚斋内景

The interior of the Hall of Accumulated Void.

题额取自《庄子》"唯道集虚",为园主颐养情性之居。斋内几乎空无一物,却充盈着浓浓的哲理意趣。

五峰书屋内景
The interior of the Five Peaks Library.

屋前屋后，均有庭院；前院后院，皆有峰峦。写意庐山五老峰，古本典籍，藏之天下名山。

五峰书屋前院一角
Part of the forecourt of the Five Peaks Library.

丹枫如染、绿叶如洗、湖石如云、在漏明墙映衬下，
倍添幽趣，更入深情。

小姐楼外间陈设
Furnishings of the outer room of the boudoir.

木刻漆屏、山水槅扇，隔出个优雅静谧、
文气氤氲的艺术空间。

外间春夏秋冬系列挂屏
A set of wall hangings in the outer room.

清宣鼎(1862—1908)画。水仙牡丹，柳湖群鸭，鹦鹉黄菊，琴鹤梅花
——写出四时季相，风格古色古香。

小姐楼外间楼廊
The veranda of the outer room.

日光穿竹，翠色玲珑、流苏垂缕，栏影成文。于此倚凭赏览，美景粲然入目。

内间闺房陈设
Furnishings of the inner room of the boudoir.

笔杆床，纱帐锦衾；玫瑰椅、妆奁鸾镜；盥器、灯台、立柜、
衣架、绣鞋、罗裙……散发出古代女性文化的芳馨。

琴

棋

闺房文化生活
Cultural pursuits inside the boudoir.

书画

女红(绣)

琴韵悠扬，棋声清亮，书画
翰墨飘香，飞针走线情意长。

看松读画轩内景
The interior of the Hall of Viewing
Pines and Contemplating Paintings.

轩前、苍松古柏如画；屏上，
群松远山似真。真与假交融成趣，
松与画相得益彰。

轩内楹联

Literary couplets.

楹联写乍暖还寒时节，摹艳冶柔绵情景，诉之视、听、嗅、肤、意诸觉；叠字回文，顺读琅琅上口，倒读铮铮悦耳，堪称天下奇联！

轩内裙板木雕
Woodcarving inside the hall.

轩内"石清供"
The ornament of petrified pine inside the hall.

松木化石

灵璧石

轩西梢间木刻书画
Wood-carved painting and calligraphy in
the sitting room on the west of the hall.

清陈鸿寿(1768-1822)作。隶书
夸张奇崛，富于装饰美；古梅郁勃苍
劲，富于金石味；填以石绿，显现一
片亮色，文采斐斐。

看松读画轩前古柏
Ancient cypresses in front of the hall.

　　已有八百高龄，铜柯石根，霜皮黛影，俯仰生姿，槎牙苍劲，倔强地超拔于高空，饱经历史沧桑，阅尽人间春色。

看松读画轩东院木瓜
The Chinese quince in the eastern court of the hall.

"投我以木瓜，报之以琼琚。"树龄二百余年的木瓜，
金果灿灿出墙，满院诗意馥郁。

小山丛桂轩内景
The interior of the Hall of Osmanthus Hill.

开敞的四面厅，装修有玲珑剔透之致，
室内有光明洞彻之美，遍收四周景色于窗棂
之内。

轩内楹联
Literary couplets.

　　清何绍基(1799 — 1873)书。"山势盘陀真
是画"，状云岗之巉岏 ；"泉流宛委遂成书"，
喻絫涧之蜿蜒。书画成双作对，取譬贴切，可
谓盖世妙联！

轩前湖石假山
The hillock in front of the hall.

瘦漏生奇，多方胜景；嵌空安巧，咫尺山林——于此可以
邀明月，可以招流云。

"铁琴"砖额，引出一则
神异动人的音乐故事……

琴室及室内挂屏
The Lute Chamber and interior wall hangings.

古琴、琴砖、琴几、挂屏……以壁山为
对景。于此抚琴动操，欲令众山皆响，琴音
与园景共鸣，大乐与天地同韵。

琴室前庭叠壁山
The rockery hill against the wall in the forecourt of the Lute Chamber.

以墙为纸，以石为绘，仿郭熙卷云皴笔意，画出"幽崖耸峙，修竹檀栾"之境界。

濯缨水阁及其水环境
The Waterside Pavilion of Washing Hat Tassel and its surroundings.

"沧浪之水清兮，可以濯吾缨。"临流画阁，轻浮于水；池岸洞穴，吞吐于水。一派水情逸韵，涟漪荡漾，谱写着渔隐的诗章。

云岗山水

The scene of the Cloud Peak.

山岩岩分绵亘起伏，水清清分淡荡铺展，绿树葱茏茂密，宛同一帧立体山水画卷。
万绿之中红一点，睡莲更鲜妍。

隔着云岗北望楼阁夜景
The night view of the northern chambers.

夜色转深沉，山岗入梦来。笙歌院落，灯火楼台，
诗酒燕集兴未衰。

池南曲蹊及池中倒影

The winding brook in the south of the pond and
reflections in water.

水池因山成曲折，山蹊随水作低平。池清平如镜，尘翳水洗净。
上下一片碧玲珑，俯仰澄情性。

引静桥
Yinjing Bridge.

如一钩新月，似一张弯弓，为中国园林精美小小石拱桥之最。与桥下的槃涧，构成小桥流水的袖珍天地。

水池东南缘墙木香

The creeping banksia rose on the wall to the
southeast of the pond.

　　小桥旁，高墙上，袅袅丛丛，带月垂香。
枝结藤缠，翠浓花繁；受雨凝云重，惹风舞雪
轻。

槃涧及其石刻
The stream and its name "Panjian" carved on stone.

　　相传为宋刻。日销月铄，风蚀苔侵，更增苍然古意深！

　　窄涧曲折，泉流宛委，萝蔓杂出，古藤垂荫，如同自然天成——于此可小中见大，浅中见深，近中见远，假中见真。

水池东北之建筑组合
The architectural group to the northeast of the pond.

立面多样、层次丰富的建筑群，高下相
倾，大小相邻，虚实相间，曲直相形……

射鸭廊、方亭一带景观
The scene of Duck-hunting Veranda and the
Square Pavilion.

优美的波形天际线下，亭廊屋宇、挂落窗槛，在粉墙背景上更见雅丽、
倒影入池、波纹摇曳，胜似宋代工致的院画小品。

蹈和馆东北篑衣械
The red maple to the northeast of the hall.

丹枫虬枝，如惊蛇之拗曲失道，似游龙之缱绻在宵；其叶则红霞层层，
绛云夕照，在曲廊朱柱辉映下分外妖娆。

蹈和馆附近曲廊
The winding corridor outside the Hall of Harmony.

游廊迤逦，随形而弯，依势而曲。引
人走向何方？走向历史时空深处。

殿春簃庭院门景
The scene through the doorframe of the
Peony Court.

门外有桥桥欲曲，山亭水轩，藏春无穷。
曲径通幽处，"真意"在其中。

冷泉亭
The Cold Spring Pavilion.

在花木峰石围拱中，冷泉亭分外气度不凡。其戗角如凤展彩翼，而墙上又
添双翅，翩翩欲飞，负载着超尘脱俗、追求自由的文士心灵。

扣之，铿然发清音；观之，黛黑隐白纹；
嵌空虚中，峭硬坚润，层棱险怪，折襞纵横；
似雄鹰之养精而将飞，蓄势而未腾。

亭内英石峰
The Ying rock inside the pavilion.

涵碧泉及周围景观
The scene highlighted by the Green
Spring.

　　湖石竞宛转，窈然一泉深。大旱
不枯，冷然渊渟。泉前铺地，网纹交
织，鱼虾相映，好一派水意渔情！

庭隅"虎儿"墓碑
The tombstone for "the Tiger Cub".

　　别梦依稀，情系故园。
国画大师张大千(1899—
1983)为仲兄所蓉虎儿题写
墓碑，自台湾遥寄姑苏。

殿春簃庭院
The Peony Court.

　　和中部水池一样，布景于周边：画堂石栏、侧廊壁山、
嘉木花坛……绿阴满地，显得疏旷雅倩，洁净清妍。

殿春簃内景
The interior of the Peony Cottage.

邵雍《芍药》诗："一声啼鸠画楼东，魏紫姚黄扫地空。多谢化工怜寂寞，尚留芍药殿春风。"殿春簃像芍药一样，绰约艳丽、温馨宜人。

籁内窗景
The picture windows of the Peony Cottage.

　　诗情、画意、乐韵，三者交响：优美
的乱纹花窗，巧作画框；窗外赖有芭蕉，
不负夜雨潇湘。

殿春籁侧书斋
The study room next to the Peony Cottage.

　　"灯火夜深书有味，墨华晨湛字生
香。"桌椅橱几，布置得体；芍药书画，点
出"殿春"之题，极富文人书卷气。

殿春簃侧书斋窗景
The picture windows of the study room.

窗外，竹石文光清影；几上、盆菊冷香幽色。
如诗如画，有情有味，令人似入芝兰之室。

张大千昆仲绘画

Paintings by artist Zhang Daqian and his brother.

黄海幽栖　张大千1935年春作于吴门网师园　　　风虎云龙　张善子1935年夏作于吴门网师园

露华馆前牡丹圃

The peony flowerbed in front of the Hall of Dewy Grace.

"云想衣裳花想容,春风拂槛露华浓",国色天香瑶圃中。
红烂熳、白婵娟、绿玲珑。春芳馥馥、韶光融融。

古典夜花园
The classical night garden.

流光溢彩，金蛇狂舞，绮罗弦管笑语；火树银花不夜园、
池塘倒影，疑入龙宫深处。

夜花园昆曲评弹演出
Kunqu Opera and local ballad singing in the night garden.

　　昆曲、评弹与园林，曾是姑苏同芳共荣的艺术姐妹。而今在网师夜花园恢复演出，赢得了中外游客赞美。

形制秀美、线条简洁的双层书几

构架谨严、形式活泼的紫檀木条桌

体型敦重、格调古雅的嵌大理石围屏弥勒榻，
五屏均刻有清阮元 (1764—1849) 题跋

构思精巧、造型挺拔的仿竹节纹多用棋桌

园藏红木家具举隅

Part of the garden's collection of mahogany furniture

清乾隆豆青出戟纹加彩诗句壁瓶

清雍正青花缠枝花卉将军罐

清道光哥窑贴花双龙耳蒜头瓶

清光绪青花五彩摆什景花卉大罐

清光绪钧红釉鸡心贯耳扁瓶

民国兰釉地粉彩花卉双羊耳八角大尊

园藏古瓷珍品举隅

The collection of antique ceramics of the garden.

网 师 园 总 平 面 图
GENERAL FLOOR PLAN OF THE MASTER-OF-NETS GARDEN

1. 大门　　　　　　*The main entrance*
2. 轿厅　　　　　　*The sedan-chair hall*
3. 大厅　　　　　　*The major reception hall*
4. 撷秀楼　　　　　*The Hall of Capturing Grace*
5. 五峰书屋　　　　*The Five Peaks Library*
6. 集虚斋　　　　　*The Hall of Accumulated Void*
7. 竹外一枝轩　　　*The Bamboo-flanked Pavilion*
8. 看松读画轩　　　*The Hall of Viewing Pines and Contemplating Paintings*
9. 殿春簃　　　　　*The Peony Cottage*
10. 风到月来亭　　　*The Pavilion of Breeze in Moon-lit Night*
11. 濯缨水阁　　　　*The Water-side Pavilion of Washing Hat Tassel*
12. 小山丛桂轩　　　*The Hall of Osmanthus Hill*
13. 露华馆　　　　　*The Hall of Dewy Grace*
14. 蹈和馆　　　　　*The Hall of Harmony*
15. 琴室　　　　　　*The Lute Chamber*
16. 梯云室　　　　　*The Hall of Cloud Stairway*
17. 瓷器馆　　　　　*Show room of antique porcelain*
18. 后门　　　　　　*The back gate*
19. 十全街　　　　　*Shiquan Street*
20. 阔家头巷　　　　*Kuojiatou Lane*

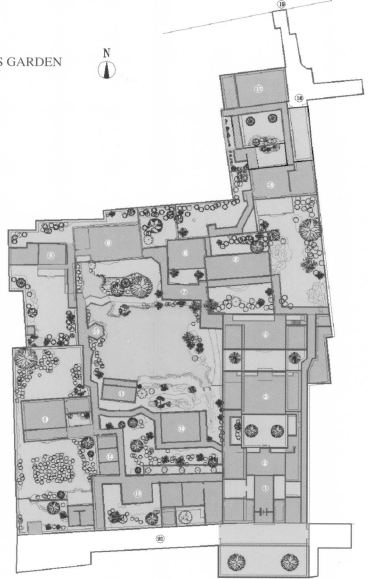

N

网师逸韵图

Sketch Map of Master-of-nets Garden

图书在版编目（CIP）数据

世界文化遗产网师园／网师园管理处编.—苏州：古吴轩出版社，2003.7
ISBN 7-80574-719-9

Ⅰ.世... Ⅱ.网... Ⅲ.①风光摄影－中国－现代－摄影集②古典园林
－苏州市－摄影集 Ⅳ.J424

中国版本图书馆 CIP 数据核字（2003）第 050960 号

顾　　问：金学智
主　　编：潘益新
编　　务：潘益新　纪辰林　王咏梅　陆桂荣
　　　　　叶松云　刘　苏　吴　元　郑可俊
撰　　文：金学智　潘益新
翻　　译：沈仲辉
摄　　影：郑可俊

责任编辑：张维明　洪　芳
装帧设计：唐伟明
责任印制：蒋家宏

世界文化遗产 网师园
出版发行：古吴轩出版社
　　　　　（苏州市憩桥巷9号）
经　　销：江苏省新华书店
印　　刷：上海界龙艺术印刷有限公司
开　　本：889×1194　1/24
印　　张：4
版　　次：2003年8月第1版
　　　　　2003年8月第1次印刷
印　　数：1—3000
书　　号：ISBN7-80574-719-9/J·562
定　　价：58.00元